NOTEBOOK

WITH QUOTATIONS INSPIRATIONAL

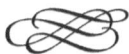

MARTIN EDEN

CONTENTS

If you are lucky enough to find a way of life you love, you have to find the courage to live it. John irving

THE SUREST WAY TO CORRUPT A
YOUTH IS TO INSTRUCT HIM TO
HOLD IN HIGHER ESTEEM THOSE
WHO THINK ALIKE THAN THOSE
WHO THINK
DIFFERENTLY.NIETZSCHE

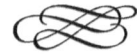

I WAS MOTIVATED TO BE DIFFERENT
IN PART BECAUSE I WAS DIFFERENT.
DONNA BRAZILE

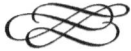

DISCOVERY CONSISTS NOT IN
SEEKING NEW LANDS BUT IN
SEEING WITH NEW EYES. MARCEL
PROUST

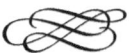

YESTERDAY I WAS CLEVER, SO I
WANTED TO CHANGE THE WORLD.
TODAY I AM WISE, SO I AM
CHANGING MYSELF. RUMI

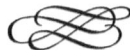

THE HAPPINESS OF YOUR LIFE
DEPENDS UPON THE QUALITY OF
YOUR THOUGHTS. MARCUS
AURELIUS

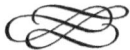

DO ONE THING A DAY THAT SCARES
YOU. ELEANOR ROOSEVELT

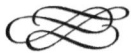

RUDENESS IS THE WEAK PERSON'S
IMITATION OF STRENGTH. ERIC
HOFFER

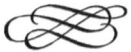

WE ARE WHAT WE REPEATEDLY DO.
ARISTOTLE

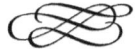

BE SO GOOD THEY CAN'T IGNORE
YOU. STEVE MARTIN

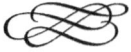

SOMETIMES YOU WILL NEVER KNOW
THE VALUE OF A MOMENT UNTIL IT
BECOMES A MEMORY. DR. SEUSS

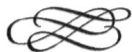

LEARN THE RULES LIKE A PRO SO
YOU CAN BREAK THEM LIKE AN
ARTIST. PABLO PICASSO

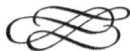

ONCE YOU CHOOSE HOPE,
ANYTHING IS POSSIBLE.
CHRISTOPHER REEVE

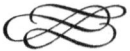

YOU MUST DO THE THING YOU
THINK YOU CANNOT DO. ELEANOR
ROOSEVELT

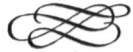

I HAVE NOT FAILED. I'VE JUST
FOUND 10.000 WAYS THAT WON'T
WORK. THOMAS EDISON

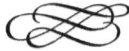

WELL DONE IS BETTER THAN WELL
SAID. BENJAMIN FRANKLIN

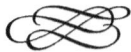

WHAT A STRANGE ILLUSION IT IS TO
SUPPOSE THAT BEAUTY IS
GOODNESS. LEO TOLSTOY

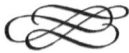

AN ESSENTIAL ASPECT OF
CREATIVITY IS NOT BEING AFRAID
TO FAIL. EDWIN LAND

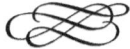

INTELLIGENCE WITHOUT AMBITION
IS A BIRD WITHOUT WINGS.
SALVADOR DALI

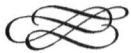

IF WE WAIT UNTIL WE ARE READY,
WE WILL BE WAITING FOR THE REST
OF OUR LIVES. LEMONY SNICKET

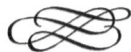

LEAP, AND THE NET WILL APPEAR.
JOHN BURROUGHS

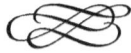

WHEREVER YOU ARE - BE ALL
THERE. JIM ELIOT

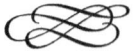

ALL OUR DREAMS CAN COME TRUE IF
WE HAVE THE COURAGE TO PURSUE
THEM. WALT DISNEY

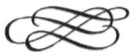

IT DOESN'T MATTER HOW SLOW YOU
GO AS LONG AS YOU DO NOT STOP.
CONFUCIUS

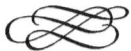

NOTHING CAN BRING YOU PEACE
BUT YOURSELF. RALPH WALDO
EMERSON

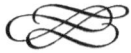

YOU MUST BE THE CHANGE YOU
WANT SEE IN THE WORLD.
MAHATMA GANDHI

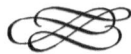

GIVE ME SIX HOURS TO CHOP DOWN
A TREE AND I WILL SPEND THE
FIRST FOUR SHARPENING THE AXE.
ABRAHAM LINCOLN

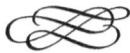

THINGS DO NOT HAPPEN. THINGS ARE MADE TO HAPPEN. JOHN F. KENNEDY

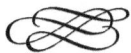

IF YOU ARE ALWAYS TRYING TO BE
NORMAL YOU WILL NEVER KNOW
HOW AMAZING YOU CAN BE. MAYA
ANGELOU

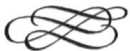

THE WEAK CAN NEVER FORGIVE.
FORGIVENESS IS THE ATTRIBUTE OF
THE STRONG. MAHATMA GANDHI

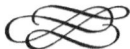

MOST FOLKS ARE AS HAPPY AS THEY
MAKE UP THEIR MINDS TO BE.
ABRAHAM LINCOLN

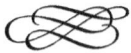

KEEP YOUR FACE ALWAYS TOWARD
THE SUNSHINE AND SHADOWS WILL
FALL BEHIND YOU. WALT WHITMAN

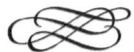

IN THE MIDST OF WINTER, I FOUND
THERE WAS, WITHIN ME, AN
INVINCIBLE SUMMER. ALBERT
CAMUS

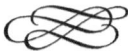

I WALK SLOWLY, BUT NEVER WALK
BACKWARD. ABRAHAM LINCOLN

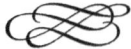

SIMPLICITY IS THE ULTIMATE FORM
OF SOPHISTICATION. LEONARDO DA
VINCI

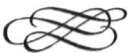

LIFE IS LIKE RIDING A BICYCLE. TO
KEEP YOUR BALANCE, YOU MUST
KEEP MOVING. ALBERT EINSTEIN

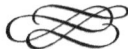

YOU CAN'T USE UP CREATIVITY. THE MORE YOU USE, THE MORE YOU HAVE. MAYA ANGELOU

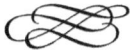

YOUTH HAS NO AGE. PABLO PICASSO

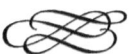

NEVER LOVE ANYBODY WHO TREATS
YOU LIKE YOU'RE ORDINARY. OSKAR
WILDE

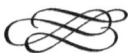

TO HAVE BEEN LOVED SO DEEPLY,
EVEN THOUGH THE PERSON WHO
LOVED US IS GONE, WILL GIVE US
SOME PROTECTION FOREVER. J. K.
ROLLING

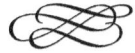

I BELIEVE THE WORLD IS AS WE
CHOOSE TO VIEW IT. SMILE AS
THAT. OUR HAPPINESS IS, IN THE
END, UP TO US, END NO ONE ELSE.
SUSAN FLETCHER

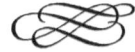

IF YOU ARE GOING THROUGH HELL,
KEEP GOING. WINSTON CHURCHILL

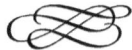

THE CURE FOR ANYTHING IS SALT
WATER- SWEAT, TEARS, OR THE SEA.
ISAK DINESEN

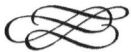

THE SUREST WAY TO CORRUPT A
YOUTH IS TO INSTRUCT HIM TO
HOLD IN HIGHER ESTEEM THOSE
WHO THINK ALIKE THAN THOSE
WHO THINK DIFFERENTLY.
NIETZSCHE

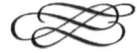

NOT TILL WE ARE LOST... DO WE
BEGIN TO FIND OURSELVES.
THOREAU

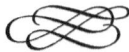

YOU HAVE TO LEARN THE RULES OF
THE GAME. AND THEN YOU HAVE TO
PLAY BETTER THAN ANYONE ELSE.
ALBERT EINSTEIN

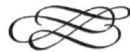

BE CURIOUS, NOT JUDGMENTAL.
WALT WHITMAN

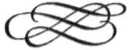

IF YOU WANT TO LIVE A HAPPY LIFE,
TIE IT TO A GOAL, NOT TO PEOPLE
OR OBJECTS. ALBERT EINSTEIN

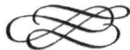

ALWAYS BE ON THE LOOKOUT FOR
THE PRESENCE OF WONDER. B. B.
WHITE

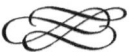

BOOKS ARE UNIQUELY PORTABLE
MAGIC. STEPHEN KING

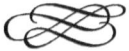

NEVER GIVE UP ON A DREAM JUST
BECAUSE OF THE TIME IT WILL TAKE
TO ACCOMPLISH IT. THE TIME WILL
PASS ANYWAY. EARL NIGHTINGALE

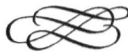

IF YOU ARE LUCKY ENOUGH TO FIND
A WAY OF LIFE YOU LOVE, YOU HAVE
TO FIND THE COURAGE TO LIVE IT.
JOHN IRVING

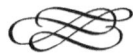

www.ingramcontent.com/pod-product-compliance
Lightning Source LLC
Chambersburg PA
CBHW020924180526

45163CB00007B/2877